# Unbelievable Pictures and Facts About Dominican Republic

By: Olivia Greenwood

# Introduction

The Dominican Republic is a highly popular country for tourists to visit. The weather is good, prices are economical and the country has beautiful scenery. Now is your chance to learn all about the wonderful country of the Dominican Republic.

# Is is a family-friendly country to visit?

The answer is a big yes. It is a very family-friendly place and family is very important. It is also a great place to bring your family on a holiday as there is literally something for everyone.

# Are there many things to buy for gifts in the Dominican Republic?

You will find many things to buy as gifts. You will be spoilt for choice. Not only does the country have some wonderful but you will find all sorts of markets and stalls to buy things.

# Are people in the Dominican Republic poor?

There is, unfortunately, a big divide between the rich people in the country and the poor. A large portion of the people in the country is extremely poor.

# What language do they speak in the country?

The main language which they speak in the country is Spanish. Although it may prove useful to know that most people can also speak fluent English.

# Are people family orientated in the Dominican Republic?

People are extremely family orientated in the Dominican Republic. Everyone looks after their family. It is very common for people to live with many extended family members.

# Which is the biggest sport in the Dominican Republic?

The sport which is played the most and loved by everyone is baseball.

# Which items are exported the most in the country?

They export all sorts of goods. The most popular things which they export are cigars, medical equipment, bananas and certain types of metals.

# Which religion is practiced the most in the Dominican Republic?

The main religion which they practice in the country is Christianity.

# Is the country a popular place for tourists to visit?

The country is a massive tourist attraction. Each year millions of people come to visit from all over the world.

# Which types of food do people eat in the country?

People eat all sorts of foods in the Dominican Republic. They have a tendency to eat lots of different meats.

# Can any unique stones be found in the Dominican Republic?

The answer is a big yes. The Dominican Republic has two specific stones which can't be found anywhere else on earth. The names of these stones are the Larimar and Dominican Amber.

# Which currency do they use in the Dominican Republic?

The current financial currency which they use is the Dominican Peso.

# Will you find any beaches in the Dominican Republic?

Of course, you will find beaches in the Dominican Republic. There are all sorts of amazing beaches.

# Which city is the capital city of the Dominican Republic?

Have you heard of Santo Domingo? This is the capital city and it is also home to millions of people.

# Will you find many animals in the Dominican Republic?

You will find many animals in the Dominican Republic. You will even find animals that can only be found in the country such as the Hispaniolan Hutia which is a very unique type of guinea pig.

# What type of weather does the country experience?

The country is known for its beautiful weather. The weather usually remains consistent throughout the year. During the summer months, it is very warm and the sun is always shining.

# Is the Dominican Republic big or small?

In terms of square miles, the Dominican Republic is 18,704. That is neither big or small in comparison to other places.

# Will you be safe when you travel in the Dominican Republic?

The good news is that it is relatively safe to travel in the Dominican Republic. However, you should always not take any unnecessary safety risks.

# What type of landscape does the Dominican Republic have?

The country has a truly stunning landscape. It has many rainforests, coastlines and mountains.

# Where in the world can you find the Dominican Republic?

Do you know where the Caribbean islands are on the map? Well, the Dominican Republic will be found there. If you want some more clues, you can look for the island of Hispaniola and you will certainly find it.

Made in the USA
Monee, IL
08 November 2020